AF615626

Duke Ellington

Richard Terrill

Chicago, Illinois

Published by Raintree, a division of Reed Elsevier, Inc.
Chicago, Illinois
Customer Service 888-363-4266
Visit our website at www.raintreelibrary.com

For information, address the publisher
Raintree, 100 N. LaSalle, Suite 1200, Chicago, IL 60602

Printed and bound in the United States by Lake Book Manufacturing, Inc.
07 06 05 04 03
10 9 8 7 6 5 4 3 2 1

Library of Congress Cataloging-in-Publication Data

Terrill, Richard, 1953-
Duke Ellington / Richard Terrill.
p. cm. -- (African American biographies)
Summary: Examines the life and career of the jazz composer, bandleader, and pianist.
Includes bibliographical references (p.) and index.
ISBN 0-7398-6869-1 (HC), 1-4109-0035-5 (Pbk.)
1. Ellington, Duke, 1899-1974--Juvenile literature. 2. Jazz musicians--United States--Biography--Juvenile literature. [1. Ellington, Duke, 1899-1974. 2. Musicians. 3. Composers. 4. Jazz. 5. African Americans--Biography.] I. Title. II. Series: African American biographies (Chicago, Ill.)
ML3930.E44 T47 2003
781.65'092--dc21

2002153358

Acknowledgments
The publishers would like to thank the following for permission to reproduce photographs:
pp. 4, 6, 10, 12, 24, 26, 28, 31, 33, 34, 37, 47, 48, 51, 54, 57, 58 Bettmann/CORBIS; pp. 8, 14, 18 CORBIS; p. 20 Hulton/Archive by Getty Images; p. 22 Hulton-Deutsch Collection/CORBIS; p. 45 Underwood & Underwood/CORBIS; p. 52 Ted Williams/CORBIS.

Cover photograph: Underwood & Underwood/CORBIS

Content Consultant
Kai Fikentscher
School of Contemporary Arts
Ramapo College of New Jersey

Some words are shown in bold, **like this.** You can find out what they mean by looking in the Glossary.

Contents

Duke Ellington posed for this picture in 1933 before departing for his first European concert tour with his orchestra.

Introduction

Duke Ellington was a famous performer and bandleader. He is also one of America's greatest **composers.** He wrote much of the music that his band, the Duke Ellington Orchestra, played.

Jazz was the music that made Duke Ellington famous. It is a type of music defined by its strong beat, or rhythm. Jazz is also an original art form invented by Americans. African Americans first played jazz in the early 1900s. Many other forms of music, such as rock, rhythm and blues, and rap, have all been influenced by jazz.

When Ellington began performing in the early 1900s, jazz was less respected in America than in Europe. Because of this, his band often played in bars and clubs, not in concert halls. Concert halls were reserved for music of European origin played by musicians who had training in music schools. Musicians who played jazz, such as Ellington, learned to play mostly from each other.

Radio helped make Duke Ellington's records popular. Here, Ellington is being a guest disk jockey (person who plays music) at a radio station.

In His Words

"A problem is a chance for you to do your best."

"I like any and all of my associations with music—writing, playing, and listening. We write and play from our perspective, and the audience listens from its perspective. If and when we agree, I am lucky."

"Playing 'bop' [**bebop**] is like playing Scrabble with all the vowels missing."

Duke Ellington helped Americans see that **jazz** was serious music, too. He and his band toured the world. People estimate that he performed about 20,000 shows during his lifetime. Ellington did more than maybe any other person to change the way Americans think about jazz. Many people became fans of jazz after hearing his music. For his achievements, Ellington won many honors near the end of his life, including nine Grammy awards.

Music was so important to Ellington that he once said, "I live with music." He wanted to write and play great, complex music that people also enjoyed listening to. Throughout his career he wrote and recorded hundreds of musical pieces. This is his lasting gift to America and to the world.

African Americans found greater opportunities for education in Washington D.C., in the early 1900s.

Chapter 1: Early Years

On April 29, 1899, Daisy Kennedy Ellington gave birth to Edward Kennedy Ellington. She and her husband, James, lived in Washington, D.C., during the years when **Jim Crow laws** enforced **segregation.** These laws in the United States separated African-American people from white people. For instance, Jim Crow laws kept blacks and whites from attending the same schools or staying in the same hotels.

In the early 1900s, segregation kept many African-Americans from finding opportunities in the South. However, Washington, D.C., was a better place to live, probably because of the availability of government jobs. Our nation's capital was one of the only cities in America where many African Americans owned stores and businesses, or were doctors, dentists, and teachers. There, African-American people could attend good schools. They enjoyed quality dance, theater, and music performances in their neighborhoods.

Ellington was well known for his skill in playing piano music. Here, he and a friend are performing for a small audience.

James was a butler for wealthy white people. For a time he even worked at the White House. The family was not rich, but they did have two pianos in their home. Little did they know how important the piano would become to their only child.

Young Edward Becomes the "Duke"

Edward's parents taught him to appreciate good art, music, and food and to practice good manners. According to one story, one of Edward's friends teased him about his good manners by calling him the "Duke." Edward enjoyed this nickname because he liked to act and speak as if he were a wealthy, important person. "I am the grand noble Duke," he said. Someday the whole world would know him by that nickname.

Edward's mother showered much attention on her only child. She thought her son would do great things, and the young Duke grew up believing that, too. Duke Ellington remained very close to his mother her whole life.

Daisy Ellington wanted her son to be active in the arts. When he was seven or eight, Edward took piano lessons from a teacher named Mrs. Clinkscales, funny as that name seems. But Edward grew restless practicing scales and drills on the piano. He liked playing baseball more. His first job was selling peanuts to people at baseball games.

Edward discovered that he had a talent for drawing. He studied commercial art at the Armstrong Manual Training School. But his career as an artist never even started. He began to lose interest in drawing after he heard the pianists like Harvey Brooks play **ragtime** music. This music had a special beat and rhythm that was created by people playing certain notes loudly. It was very different from the piano scales and drills he had learned as a child. Edward dropped out of school to become a piano player instead.

Duke Ellington and his band were so popular that they were in some movies. This scene is from the movie Cabin in the Sky, *1943.*

Piano Player

Instead of going to another school to learn music, Ellington learned how to play from other musicians. Harvey Brooks was one of his first teachers, showing him how to do some piano tricks. Other musicians taught him even more and helped him learn to read **sheet music.** As his skills improved, he began playing the piano in different places around the city. Television, radio, and record players had not been invented yet. People heard music only when someone like Duke performed it live.

In 1917, Duke formed his first band and called it "Duke's Serenaders." Duke found he was good at finding many places for his band to play and make money. The band played at different balls and parties around the Washington, D.C., and Virginia areas.

Between 1918 and 1919, Duke's personal life changed forever. He moved into his own house. He also fell in love with and married a woman named Edna Thompson. On March 11, 1919, his only son, Mercer Kennedy Ellington, was born. Now Duke had to earn money for his new family. He did this by playing even more shows.

Soon, Duke Ellington was playing all over Washington, D.C., for both white audiences and black audiences. He worked with musicians who played the banjo, drums, and saxophone, playing a new music popular with dancers, called **ragtime.** Ellington began to write and perform his own ragtime songs. His band became very popular.

On most nights, Duke's Serenaders had more offers to play than they could take, so Ellington hired more musicians and formed several bands, sending them out to play in different places at the same time. In this way, his reputation spread, and he earned even more money. Duke Ellington was not only a great musician, but a very good businessperson. It was his talent as a businessperson that eventually made him decide to leave Washington, D.C.

Ellington moved to Harlem and was a part of the Harlem Renaissance. He and his band played in many Harlem clubs.

Chapter 2: Harlem

Ellington could have stayed in Washington, D.C., with his family and continue to work with Duke's Serenaders. But he knew that in New York City he would have a chance to be even more successful, especially in a part of town called Harlem.

Back in the 1910s, African Americans from all over the country were moving to Harlem. Important writers such as Langston Hughes and Zora Neale Hurston lived there. So did important thinkers, like W.E.B. Dubois, who started the NAACP (National Association for the Advancement of Colored People). People in Harlem spread the idea that black people should be proud of themselves and their culture. Culture is the way people live together in a place and time. It also means the art they make, such as books and music. This rise of art and politics in this place and at this time became known as the **Harlem Renaissance.**

The word *renaissance* is the French word for "rebirth." Music, too, was being reborn in Harlem. It was a new music called **jazz.** Jazz started in New Orleans when black musicians there were allowed to study **classical** music that came from Europe. Thus, we say that jazz is made up of at least two things: the rhythm, or beat, of earlier black music, and the harmony of classical musical. (Harmony is the pleasing way the sounds are put together.)

The Washingtonians Play in Harlem

Jazz was more complex than the **ragtime** that Duke Ellington played in Washington, D.C. One main feature of jazz was that players would **improvise** solos. This means they would make up the tune of the music on the spot. People could dance to jazz if they wanted to, but it was not meant only for dancing. It was music that could just be listened to for the sake of its beauty and form.

Ellington came to New York in 1922 with some musician friends. One of them was a drummer named Sonny Greer who would play with Duke Ellington for many years. At first, Ellington did not play much and had difficulty making a living. One day Ellington found fifteen dollars lying in the street. He and his friends used the money to go back home to Washington, D.C.

In 1923, they returned to New York and formed a band called "The Washingtonians." They had better luck in Harlem this time, playing steadily for four years. True, they had to play in a dark

The Harlem Renaissance

In the years right after World War I (1914–1918), many African Americans left the South for northern cities such as Washington, D.C., Chicago, and the Harlem section of New York City. They were mostly looking for better jobs and hoping to escape racism in the South. However, these new communities also led African Americans to think more about what it meant to be black in America. Thinkers and leaders such as Alain LeRoy Locke, W.E.B. DuBois, and Marcus Garvey encouraged African Americans to take pride in their heritage. Writers like Langston Hughes and Zora Neale Hurston wrote about the experiences of African-Americans. Painters and musicians also worked and lived here. Because of this, the 1920s in New York came to be known as the **Harlem Renaissance.**

basement called the Hollywood Club. The stage was so small that not everyone could fit on it. Duke played piano while sitting on the dance floor. Even so, the young musicians worked and learned.

When trumpet player "Bubber" Miley joined the band, he taught the other members a lesson in jazz. Bubber was not as good a trumpet player as some others in New York, but his style was like no one else's. He used a **mute.** This is a cup held over the end of the horn, which made the trumpet make "wah wah" sounds when he played. Miley knew how to **improvise** the new music of **jazz** to get in touch with listeners.

Ellington is composing music. He listened to his band members play and tried to write parts that suited each musician.

Duke was smart to add Miley to his group, and he would continue to make wise decisions throughout his career as a bandleader. Many of his musicians stayed with his band for many years. Other bands usually had trouble keeping musicians.

Duke wrote music for his bandmembers. He knew the talents of each of his musicians and what would sound best. His players each added a unique sound to the music. Together, they made what was called "the Ellington sound," which was smooth, lively, and always interesting.

Becoming Popular

Soon the Washingtonians had a weekly radio show. Every Wednesday afternoon at 3:45 they would play music in the Hollywood Club. These shows were broadcast, so people all around New York could listen on their radios. Ellington's songs began to be published. Fans could buy the **sheet music** to the songs he wrote, and play them on the piano at home. Duke Ellington and his musicians became popular enough to be hired at better places with more room.

Most important, Ellington's band started making records of his own songs. In 1926, they recorded "East St. Louis Toodle-oo." In it, we can hear how Duke's music is more interesting and complex than the other **jazz** records of the times. The song seems to come in different sections that surprise us as we listen. And the trumpet of Bubber Miley seems to cry and growl and laugh. Some bands today still play "East St. Louis Toodle-oo," Ellington's first masterpiece.

Langston Hughes, an African-American writer and central figure to the Harlem Renaissance, poses by his typewriter.

Langston Hughes

Langston Hughes was born in 1902. He was an African-American writer who lived at about the same time as Duke Ellington and who wrote in many forms. He was a novelist, short-story writer, newspaper columnist, and playwright, but was most known for his poetry. His poems were not written in the style of the day, which followed the practice of earlier poets, especially famous British poets. Instead, he wrote free verse that did not rhyme. His poems were true to the African-American experience. He was especially interested in **jazz** and blues, and these forms of music were the subject of many poems. He sometimes even used the rhythm of this music in his poetry. Hughes' work made him a central figure in the **Harlem Renaissance.** He wrote and read his poetry in Harlem and influenced many other writers and artists. Later, he told about his life during the Harlem Renaissance in his autobiography. This book helps people understand what that artistic movement was like. Hughes died on May 22, 1967, after undergoing stomach surgery.

Ellington later said that "Toodle-oo" was a phrase that describes how African-American men used to limp home from the fields after a day of work. A lot of Ellington's music was inspired by the experience of African Americans.

The Cotton Club was the most exclusive club of the Harlem Renaissance. Many famous African-American musicians performed there.

Chapter 3: The Cotton Club

By 1926, Ellington's band was popular enough to attract the interest of Irving Mills. He was a well-known manager and music publisher who helped the careers of several famous **jazz** musicians, like Cab Calloway. Mills became Ellington's manager and helped him publish music. With Mills's help, the band recorded more records and published more songs as **sheet music.** More people, both white and black, came to know about the band.

In 1927, Ellington's band was given the job as house band at the most famous club in Harlem, the Cotton Club. It was the dream of many black musicians to play there. Because of **segregation,** African-American musicians were not allowed to play at concert halls. The Cotton Club was the most important and famous place they could play.

People dance at a New Year's Eve party at the Cotton Club in 1933.

One former Cotton Club bandleader described it as "a huge room. The bandstand was a replica of a southern mansion, with large white columns and a backdrop painted with weeping willows and slave quarters. Down a few steps was the dance floor, which was also used for the shows. The waiters and waitresses were dressed in red tuxedos, like butlers in a southern mansion."

All night the Cotton Club put on shows with singers, dancers, and entertainers. These performers were black, while the audience was all white people. When white people came to Harlem, the black part of the city, they heard music different from what they were used to. It moved fast and had a lively rhythm.

Members of the Band

Duke Ellington was now playing in the most famous nightclub in the largest city in America. He was able to add more musicians to his band. He began calling it the Duke Ellington Orchestra. Again, he made wise choices. "Tricky Sam" Nanton had joined the band on trombone. Like Bubber Miley, Nanton had a very unique style of playing. People who listened to the records could recognize Nanton's playing.

Barney Bigard joined Ellington's band on clarinet. He came from New Orleans, where **jazz** was born, and played in the style of that city. Two new saxophone players in the band would remain with Ellington for many years. Harry Carney played baritone saxophone, the largest of the saxophones in a band. It was unusual for someone to **improvise** solos on this big horn as well as Carney.

Johnny Hodges played the alto saxophone, which led the saxophones in a band. Hodges could play fast, but could also play beautiful slow melodies. He played with Duke Ellington for most of his life, until the 1960s, and became one of the most famous alto saxophone players ever.

Ellington never actually met President Herbert Hoover during his first visit to the White House. He just had this picture taken outside.

The Cotton Club gave Duke opportunities as a bandleader. Other bands in other clubs played mostly for people dancing. But every night, Duke had to play music to go with all kinds of singers, performers, and comedians. He got a chance to write different kinds of music. Some of it was music that people needed to listen to carefully, as they would in a concert hall. So Ellington's music continued to become more complex and more interesting.

Ellington continued to write with each player in his band in mind. He let Hodges shine on slow melodies. He wrote high notes for Carney, which sounded unusual on his very low-pitched saxophone. Nanton and Miley could express emotions and moods through the sounds they played on their horns.

Growing Fame

Ellington's music kept becoming more popular. By this time radio stations joined together into networks, such as NBC and CBS. Therefore, people all over the country could tune in their radios to hear broadcasts from the Cotton Club, five or six nights a week.

In 1927, the first movies with sound were made. Before that, all films had been silent. In 1929, Duke Ellington and his orchestra played in a 19-minute movie, *Black and Tan,* one of the first movies to include **jazz** music.

Ellington wanted listeners to think of him as a true artist, not just a bandleader. That was starting to happen. By the mid-1930s, he led the most popular African-American orchestra in America.

Racism placed some limits on his fame. In 1931, Ellington was invited to meet the U.S. President, Herbert Hoover. It would be the first time an African-American entertainer met the president in the White House. The meeting never took place. No one knows for sure why not. Ellington's picture was taken outside the White House, alone.

This picture was taken in 1934 when Duke Ellington was traveling around the country with his band.

Chapter 4: On the Road

Being a bandleader was tougher than many people realized. Duke Ellington needed to be a boss to a group of a dozen musicians, and had to make enough money to pay his players and keep his band together.

In 1929 the **Great Depression** (1929–1939) began. More than 25 percent of Americans had no job, and **poverty** spread through the country. Record sales dropped.

In 1931, Duke decided to leave the Cotton Club. He took his band on the road to tour. With less money coming from record sales, these performances helped keep the band together. The band toured the country in a series of "one nighters." This meant that the band would play one night in a ballroom in one city, then leave the next morning for another city.

Ellington traveled this way for much of his life. He said he never really owned a house that he called his home. His home was on the road. One musician said that after he left Ellington's band, he slept for an entire year.

In the early 1930s, these tours let people see the Ellington band live. Most of these dancers and listeners had only heard the band on record or on national radio broadcasts.

The tours were wildly successful. But they were important for other reasons, too. Ellington took his orchestra to the Deep South, where racism was common. Ellington's band showed others that people of different races could be friends and work together as a team. The band was made up of black musicians, except for one. Juan Tizol, a trombone player, was Puerto Rican. When the band made movies, studio bosses sometimes made Tizol, who looked white, wear black makeup. Some people in the South, and in other places in America, did not want to see a white person on stage with blacks.

Ellington's band traveled by Pullman train cars, cars that had beds in them. Band members could sleep and eat on the train. They did not have to worry about being turned away by the restaurants and hotels owned by whites in the days of **Jim Crow laws.**

Ellington also took his band to England and then to other countries in Europe. In the 1930s, Ellington's musicians were

Duke Ellington poses with his band in 1931.

surprised by the way Europeans treated them better than whites did in America. In England, the Prince of Wales sat in with Ellington's band, playing the drums for fun. He was a fan of **jazz** and of Duke Ellington. In his later years, Ellington would travel the world as a musical **ambassador** for America, someone who represented his country.

People everywhere were impressed that Ellington's musicians had no **sheet music** with them on stage. Each of the players had memorized his part. This was possible because the band played so often. It also tells us about the way Duke worked. He composed music not for musical instruments, but for individual musicians. This made it easier for the musicians to memorize their parts.

The Great Composer

Ellington is one of the greatest American **composers.** He did not always write music while sitting at the piano, like most composers. Instead, he made music together with his band, and that music sometimes was not written down until years later. Duke would tell each member what to play, modeling the music for him on the piano. The band would play the music back to him, together. He would listen to how that music sounded and take suggestions from his musicians. Then, he would make changes and again tell each player what to play. He did this until he had a sound he liked.

"If it sounds good . . . it is good," Ellington was known to say. He also called himself "the world's greatest listener" because he listened to his band members and wrote what sounded best when they played. Duke wrote music by trial and error.

Duke Ellington had a talent for writing unusual music. For example, "Mood Indigo" was a hit record in 1931 and is still often played today. In this famous song, Ellington had a clarinet, a trumpet, and a trombone play the melody together. The song was

Even when relaxing, Ellington had a hard time tearing himself away from music. This picture shows him composing music.

very simple, but it was odd to have three different instruments play the main tune. The trumpet and trombone used **mutes.** This made the song sound dark and strange (The word "indigo" means a deep blue). The clarinet is a high-pitched instrument, but Ellington wrote the music for it below the notes of the trumpet. This way, the sound of the three horns blended together.

Benny Goodman and Gene Krupa were among the most famous swing players in the big-band era of the 1930s and 1940s.

Chapter 5: The Swing Era

The 1930s is often called the **Swing** Era. Swing is a simpler form of **jazz** with a rhythm that's loose and flowing. The beat moves steadily forward in a way that made people want to dance. Swing became very popular. So, "big bands" toured the country playing swing music for people to dance to. Big bands were larger than the combos that played in the 1920s.

Jazz was becoming more popular now with white audiences, partly because more of the big bands playing swing music were white. Glenn Miller, Tommy Dorsey, and Benny Goodman (who called himself the "King of Swing") were among the popular white bandleaders. With a few exceptions, these bandleaders hired only white musicians.

Duke Ellington had been ahead of his time. His band remained somewhat popular through the 1930s. However, the white bands became even more popular. The **swing** music these white bands (and some all-black bands) played was quite simple. Often it repeated the same pattern of notes with few changes over a whole song. The music was meant to be easy and fun to dance to.

At the same time, Ellington's music was becoming more complex. Listeners who loved the swing bands sometimes did not understand or appreciate his music because it was not as easy to dance to. Thus, the 1930s were a difficult time for Duke. His players could swing hard if they wanted to, but as Ellington himself said, "**Jazz** is music; swing is business." He meant that he was willing to play dance music to make money, but he also wanted to make music that might challenge listeners. Besides being popular, he wanted to write music that would last.

Another Challenge

In 1935 Ellington's beloved mother, Daisy, died of cancer. He had brought her to New York to live with him, had bought her expensive clothes and jewelry, and had always listened to her advice. She had raised his son while he was on the road. Duke Ellington was a charming man who was liked by people from all walks of life, but his mother was always the most important person in the world for him.

For a time after her death, he found he could not write music, and he became depressed. "I have no ambition left," he said. The next year, when swing music was wildly popular, Ellington made very few recordings.

These people are dancing to swing music at a big band dance hall show.

Several factors helped Ellington get over the loss of his mother and go on. One of these factors was probably the self-confidence that his mother had taught him at an early age.

Then, in 1938 there was a lucky encounter.

Billy Strayhorn

After a performance in Pittsburgh, Philadelphia, a young African-American man came up and asked if he could show Ellington some of his **compositions.** A composition is a written work of music. Billy Strayhorn was 23, and worked in a drugstore. Unlike Ellington, Strayhorn had studied music in school. Ellington was a great judge of musicians and recognized the genius of Strayhorn right away.

One song young Strayhorn played was a favorite of the famous bandleader. "Lush Life" had a haunting, weary melody. It sounded like a song written by an older person, tired from life. How could someone so young know so much about music and life? Strayhorn's music already had the depth that Ellington sought.

Ellington asked Billy Strayhorn to come to New York. Within a year, he was writing and arranging music for Ellington's band. An **arranger** is someone who takes another person's music and decides which notes each instrument will play. Sometimes the two men would work together on writing and arranging.

Billy Strayhorn and Duke Ellington were opposite personalities. Even so, Strayhorn understood "the Ellington Sound." The partnership, and the friendship, between Ellington and Strayhorn was very close. Sometimes, it was hard to tell which of the two men had written a piece of music. "Take the A Train" is the one song people most often connect with the Duke Ellington

Ellington and Billy Strayhorn work together to write and arrange a piece of music.

Orchestra. However, it was written by Strayhorn, not Ellington.

Strayhorn was unselfish, patient, and steady. His formal musical training went along well with Ellington's sense of what sounded good. The four years after they met were among the most productive in Ellington's long career. Their partnership is among the greatest in the history of American music.

These African-American singers were among many musicians drafted to fight World War II.

Chapter 6: Facing Change

In 1941, America entered World War II (1939–1945), bringing great changes to the country and the Duke Ellington Orchestra.

The world of **jazz** changed, too. Suddenly trains were filled with soldiers, not travelers, and gasoline was in short supply. Travel became difficult for the big bands. People had less time and money to go to dance halls. On top of that, many musicians were drafted into the military to fight the Germans and the Japanese.

In 1942, the musicians' union called a strike against record companies to make more money. Most bandleaders agreed not to make new recordings, which hurt the bands because people could not hear their new music.

Many important musicians left Ellington's band during the 1940s. They were tired of travel and hoped to do better on their own. Both Barney Bigard, the clarinet player from New Orleans, and Juan Tizol, the trombone player from Puerto Rico, left after fifteen years. Ellington's singer, Ivie Anderson, also left.

Carnegie Hall

Late in 1942, Ellington was asked to play at Carnegie Hall in New York. Up until this time, Carnegie Hall had been mostly reserved for **classical** music. Classical music is the older European and, later, American music played in concerts by large orchestras with many violins and other string instruments. At the time, classical music was considered "serious" music, while **jazz** was not. Only a few jazz bands had ever played Carnegie Hall.

Duke Ellington had been trying to write "serious" jazz music for some years. This meant writing music that was longer than the typical popular song, which lasted only a few minutes. It also meant music in which all the notes were written down so that any good musicians could play it. No one had ever written a long piece of jazz music before. How would Ellington build a long piece of jazz to be played in a concert hall, not a dance hall? How would he write out solos that would still sound like jazz?

Ellington decided to write a piece of program music. Program music means the music tries to describe or be about something specific in the real world. He decided to write about the experience of African-Americans. He called the piece, written in three parts, "Black, Brown, and Beige."

Duke Ellington's skill landed him a show in Carnegie Hall in 1943.

Black, Brown, and Beige

In the first part of "Black, Brown, and Beige," the music tried to suggest the lives of African slaves in America. The second part suggested the participation of blacks in America's wars. And the third part was a hopeful piece about the twentieth century and **integration.** Integration means ending **segregation** and having black and white people live together equally.

In "Black, Brown, and Beige," Ellington continued to write to the strengths of his musicians. He gave the saxophone player Johnny Hodges the haunting melody of "Come Sunday," a section about slaves resting on the day they were allowed to go to church and pray. It may be the most beautiful melody Ellington ever wrote. "B, B, and B," as Ellington called the piece, contains his most advanced writing up to that point.

But a lot of music critics did not like the music. They said the different parts of the **composition** did not work together. Some important critics thought that **jazz** trying to be serious music was a bad idea.

Maybe this response is because the critics of **classical** music did not understand the music of African Americans. Perhaps they thought jazz was music to dance to and nothing more. Some people may not have liked the idea of African Americans playing at Carnegie Hall.

Ellington began writing down jazz music. He created longer pieces of complex music, elevating jazz to a more serious art form.

To this day, music critics disagree about "Black, Brown, and Beige." But some consider the piece to be among the best work of Duke Ellington's career and the most important long piece of **jazz**.

On January 23, 1943, Carnegie Hall was filled for a special performance. There, that night, Duke Ellington first played "Black, Brown, and Beige." Eleanor Roosevelt, the wife of the president, was there. During the evening, some famous musicians gave Duke Ellington a plaque for his achievements. Aaron Copland, the most famous American **classical composer** of the time, signed the plaque. So did Benny Goodman, the white bandleader of the most famous **swing** band.

Aaron Copland, a famous American composer, respected Ellington and his accomplishments. He signed an award plaque that was given to Ellington.

Some people thought that Ellington should break up his big band because not as many people were going to concerts.

Chapter 7: Ellington at Newport

Things remained difficult for the big bands after the end of World War II. People began listening to different kinds of music. Popular singers like Frank Sinatra left the big bands and made records on their own. Black audiences listened to a new kind of music called rhythm and blues. In the world of **jazz, bebop** was the popular new sound. Very fast and almost all **improvised,** it was played by groups of four or five musicians, not big bands of fifteen or more.

By the 1950s, television had become the most popular form of entertainment. People did not go out as much to hear music. They listened less to their radios, too, so the bands reached fewer people. It was also becoming more expensive for the bands to travel. Because of this, most of the big bands broke up. In a few years, rock-and-roll music would sweep the country.

There was pressure on Ellington to break up his band, too. For several years, he did not make much money. Then in 1951, Johnny Hodges, Ellington's most famous soloist, and Sonny Greer, the drummer who had been with Duke since Washington, D.C., left the band.

The Newport Jazz Festival

In 1954, the Newport **Jazz** Festival began. It was the first festival in which audiences sat outdoors in a beautiful setting to listen to music. (Festivals like this have become very popular.) Ellington was invited to perform at the third Newport Festival. On July 7, 1956, his band was scheduled to close the show.

It was almost midnight when the Ellington Orchestra took the stage at the end of the program. The second piece the band performed was one that the audience recognized, called "**Diminuendo** and **Crescendo** in Blue." Diminuendo means simply the music grows quieter. Crescendo means the music grows louder.

Ellington's band had been in a low period for several years, but they created a sensation that night with "Diminuendo and Crescendo." It is true that the piece, written in 1937, was not a new work. So, the excitement was not for a new Ellington **composition.**

However, because of the **improvisation** of the players, a jazz song is different every time it is performed. We can listen to the

Ellington continued to play at the Newport Jazz Festival, even into his seventies.

recording of the performance and hear the excitement on stage. First, the band plays the music together. They sound like an old swing band from the 1930s, making the music move forward in the smooth way that swing does.

After the band plays the music together, a soloist begins to **improvise.** He is Paul Gonsalves on the tenor saxophone. Ellington put this piece on the program as a chance for Gonsalves to "stretch out," as musicians say. That means his solo can go on much longer than usual.

Paul Gonsalves played 27 choruses on his tenor saxophone during the Newport show.

Gonsalves played chorus after chorus. A chorus is a musical division, meaning one time through the song. Ellington began to clap and grunt in time as Gonsalves played. By about the sixth chorus, the audience began to clap and yell in excitement. Some women got up to dance in the aisles. The man who ran the festival yelled at Duke to stop the band, afraid there would be a riot.

But the solo went on. The drums and string bass slapped harder at the beat. Ellington played behind them on piano. The audience whistled, screamed, shouted, and clapped. Paul Gonsalves played 27 choruses! Many in the audience said it was the most exciting performance they had ever heard.

The next month, Duke Ellington's picture was on the cover of *Time* magazine. His next record album, *Ellington at Newport,* was his all-time biggest seller.

Ellington received many awards later in life. Here, he is making a speech after being elected into the Swedish Music Academy, March 12, 1971.

Chapter 8: The Highest Honor

Some artists do their best work when they are very young and eager for fame. Others do their best work when they are older and experienced.

After the Newport **Jazz** Festival, Duke Ellington was popular again. Jazz had changed, and his big band would never again be the most important band in jazz. But for the rest of his life, Ellington got great recognition. He was an elder in jazz, one of its most important and best-loved figures.

Ellington had been on the jazz scene longer than just about anyone. He played big band jazz before the **Swing** Era. Among all the Swing-Era bands, Ellington's was the only one never to break up. This was a testament to his leadership and his devotion to his players.

Ellington was given more chances to shine after Newport. In the late 1950s, he was asked to write the music for a Hollywood movie called *Anatomy of a Murder*, an opportunity rarely given to African Americans at that time. Television also featured Duke Ellington. In 1957, he wrote and read the words to an hour-long music and dance show called "A Drum is a Woman." It told the story of **jazz** and featured some of his band members. It was one of the first programs to include only African-American performers.

Ellington continued his life on the road. In the 1960s, he returned to Europe, which he had visited many times. But he also went to countries where jazz was new. These were countries like Japan, India, Russia, and the countries of Latin America and Eastern Europe. Everywhere, jazz was recognized as the best of American music.

Ellington was something like an **ambassador** for his nation. An ambassador is someone who represents a government in a foreign country. But Ellington was not an ambassador who spoke for the government. He was an ambassador who spoke with music for the people of the United States.

Sacred Music

Ellington's old songs remained popular. But in his last years, he also continued to write longer **compositions.** His "Concert of Sacred Music" was first performed in San Francisco in 1965.

Duke Ellington is leading his orchestra at a Sacred Concert in the Cathedral of Saint John the Divine in New York City.

Ellington grew more religious later in his life. He thought of this sacred music as in some ways his most personal and important work. The Sacred Concerts were made up of several pieces of religious music. Some were old, and some were new. As with "Black, Brown, and Beige," critics disagreed about the success of the Sacred Concerts. Some thought they were neither jazz nor **classical.** Some thought jazz could not be religious music. Others found these concerts remarkable.

President Nixon presented the Presidential Medal of Freedom to Duke Ellington at his seventieth birthday celebration in 1969.

America's Greatest Composer

Ellington kept playing music as he got older. On May 24, 1974, he died of cancer. He was 75 years old. After his death, his son Mercer took over his band.

Ellington received many awards later in life. He was given **honorary** doctor of music degrees from universities like Yale and Howard University. Howard was a mostly African-American university in his hometown of Washington, D.C.

In 1969, Ellington was invited to the White House for his 70th birthday. Famous politicians and musicians were on the guest list for the event. That night, President Nixon presented Duke Ellington with the Presidential Medal of Freedom, the highest award an American could receive from his country. Ellington said there was no place he would rather be except in his mother's arms.

Ellington then gave a speech, using the words of his old partner Billy Strayhorn, who had died a few years before. Strayhorn had written of four freedoms that people should measure up to.

“Freedom from hate,” was one of them, Ellington said. “Freedom from self-pity (even throughout all the pain and bad news). Freedom from fear of possibly doing something that might help another more than it might help himself. And freedom from the kind of pride that could make a man feel he was better than his brother or neighbor."

This night marked perhaps the peak of his success. After he spoke, the famous and important guests at the White House applauded him. He sat down at the piano and played, and all there listened to the great **composer,** recognized at last for being a very important American artist.

Glossary

ambassador person who represents his or her own country while being in another country

arranger someone who takes another person's music and decides which notes each instrument will play

bebop type of jazz first played in the 1940s by black musicians. It was very fast and wild music.

classical music from Europe and, later, America that is typically played in concert halls by orchestras and similar groups

composer someone who writes music

composition piece of written music

crescendo musical term that describes music getting louder

diminuendo musical term that describes music getting softer

Great Depression the years from 1929 to 1939, when millions of Americans were jobless and homeless

Harlem Renaissance term used to describe a historical period which took place in Harlem, New York City, between 1925-1929, when the African-American arts community was active, producing great works of literature, art and music

honorary anything given to a person to honor him or her. The person does not have to go through the usual steps to get the award.

improvisation act of improvising

improvise in jazz, the action of making up and playing music on the spot. The music is not written down ahead of time.

integration act of white and black people being brought together in public places like schools and restaurants

jazz form of American music started by African Americans in the early twentieth century. It has a clear beat, and its main element is improvisation

Jim Crow laws laws that kept white and black people separated

mute kind of plug that horn players put in the bell (end) of their horns to muffle and soften the sound

poverty state of being very poor and not being able to afford the most basic things needed to live

ragtime style of music with a strong, syncopated rhythm

segregation actions and rules, such as Jim Crow laws, that separated African Americans from white people

sheet music music compositions printed on unbound sheets of paper so that people can play the songs on an instrument

Timeline

1899	Edward Kennedy Ellington born April 29 in Washington, D.C.
1918	Works as a band leader and piano player in Washington.
1923	Returns to New York. Plays with "The Washingtonians."
1927	Begins four-year stay at the Cotton Club in Harlem.
1928	Alto saxophonist Johnny Hodges joins the band.
1931	Begins touring the country.
1935	Ellington's mother, Daisy Ellington, dies.
1939	Meets long-time composing partner Billy Strayhorn.
1943	First performance of "Black, Brown, and Beige" at Carnegie Hall.
1951	Three important players leave the band, including Johnny Hodges and Sonny Greer.
1956	Performs at the Newport **Jazz** Festival.
1959-1960	Writes the music for the films *Anatomy of a Murder* and *Paris Blues.*
1965	First Sacred Concert in San Francisco.
1967	Billy Strayhorn dies.
1969	Presented with the Presidential Medal of Freedom by President Nixon.
1973	Publishes his autobiography.
1974	Duke Ellington dies on May 24, in New York City.

Further Information

Further reading

Brown, Gene. *Duke Ellington: Jazz Master.* Farmington Hills, Mich.: Gale Group, 2001.

Collier, James Lincoln. *Duke Ellington*. New York: Macmillan, 1991.

Collier, James Lincoln. *Jazz: An American Saga.* New York: Henry Holt, 1997.

Venezia, Mike. *Duke Ellington*. Danbury, Conn.: Scholastic, 1996.

Addresses

Duke Ellington Society
PO Box 31
Church Street Station
New York, NY 10008-0031

International Association for Jazz Education
PO Box 724
Manhattan, KS 66505

MENC: The National Association for Music Education
1806 Robert Fulton Drive
Reston, VA 20191

Smithsonian Anacostia Museum & Center for African American History and Culture
1901 Fort Place, SE
Washington, DC 20020

Index

Gill Memorial Library
29347
Terrill, Richard
Duke Ellington
J B ELL